# LIGHT *and* COLOUR

MAKING SENSE *of* SCIENCE

Peter Riley

W
FRANKLIN WATTS
LONDON • SYDNEY

First published in 2005 by Franklin Watts
96 Leonard Street, London EC2A 4XD

Franklin Watts Australia
45-51 Huntley Street, Alexandria, NSW 2015

Editors: Kate Newport, Andrew Solway
Art director: Jonathan Hair
Designer: Mo Choy
Illustrator: Ian Thompson

Picture credits:
Russ Bishop/Stock Connection/Alamy: 28.
Chris Daniels/Corbis: 4t.
Dynamics Graphics Group/Alamy: 20.
Freelance Consulting Services Pty Ltd/Corbis: 11t.
Jeff Greenberg/Alamy: 27t.
Peter Harholdt/Corbis: 19b.
Craig Lovell/Corbis: 5c.
NASA: 9b, 11b, 28b.
Troy & Mary Parlee/Alamy: 10t.
Clayton J. Price/Corbis: front cover inset.
Andrew Syred/Science Photo Library: 6t.
Bill Varie/Corbis: 19c.
Charles D. Winter/Science Photo Library: 6b.
David Woodfall/Still Pictures: front cover main, 1.

Picture research: Diana Morris

All other photography by Ray Moller.

A CIP catalogue record for this book
is available from the British Library.

ISBN 0 7496 5526 7

Printed in Malaysia

# CONTENTS

**LIVING** WITH **LIGHT**      4

**LIGHT SOURCES**      6

**THE PATH** OF **LIGHT**      8

**SHADOWS**      10

**THE COLOURS** IN **LIGHT**      12

A **CLOSER LOOK** AT **COLOUR**      14

**REFLECTING LIGHT**      16

**CURVED MIRRORS**      18

**BENDING LIGHT**      20

**LENSES**      22

**THE EYE**      24

**CAPTURING LIGHT**      26

**THE SPEED** OF **LIGHT**      28

**TIMELINE**      30

**GLOSSARY**      31

**INDEX**      32

# LIVING WITH LIGHT

**Look out of the window. If it is daylight, the scene is lit by sunlight. If it is night, the scene might be lit by street lights. There are also the tiny, twinkling lights of stars in the night sky, and sometimes the stronger light of the Moon.**

Light is a kind of energy. It travels through the air and through space in the form of tiny waves that are far too small to see. Light is very important to us and it is impossible to imagine life without it. In fact, without light from the Sun there would be no life on Earth, because plants rely on light to make food (see opposite page).

## STRAIGHT AND BENT

Put your hand in front of a torch beam and you will see that your hand obstructs the light (it cannot shine around your hand). This shows that light travels in straight lines. However, you can change the direction of a beam of light by reflecting it. Light is reflected from many surfaces, but a shiny surface reflects best.

Light can pass from one transparent substance to another. When it does so, the light bends (changes direction) by a process called refraction.

When sunlight shines through breaks in the clouds, we see beams of light like these. This shows us that light travels in straight lines.

## MAKE A LIGHT BEAM

Fill two glass beakers with water. Add a teaspoon of cold cooking oil to one beaker and stir it up. Shine a torch through the beaker of water and then through the beaker with the oil droplets in it. When can you see a light beam?

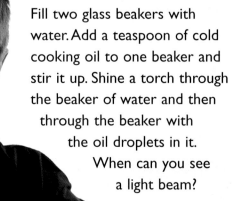

## TURN THE CORNER

Put a mirror at the corner of a thick book. Make the room dark and shine a torch along one side of the book. Can you make the light beam turn a corner by reflection?

## RAINBOWS

We may think of sunlight as a bright, white light, but really it is made from many different colours. If the Sun is shining from behind you as you watch rain falling, the raindrops reflect and refract the light so it splits up to make the bands of colours we call a rainbow.

## PLANTS AND LIGHT

The leaves of plants are packed with a green pigment called chlorophyll. The pigment captures energy from sunlight, and the plant uses this energy to make food from carbon dioxide in the air and water in the soil. Nearly all other life on Earth depends on the food that plants make. Animals either eat plants directly, or eat plant-eating animals. So all the energy we get from food comes originally from sunlight.

Rainbows always form an arc in the sky.

## SWAPPING GASES

Jan Ingenhousz (1730–1799), a Dutch scientist, performed experiments showing that plants take in carbon dioxide and give out oxygen when light shines on them. Other scientists followed his discovery by performing more experiments showing that plants use light, carbon dioxide and water to make food. Today we call this process photosynthesis.

## SEEING LIGHT

Human beings rely particularly on light – sight is a very important sense (see pages 24–25). Our eyes and our brains use light coming in from all around us to build up a picture of the outside world. Eighty per cent of the information received by seeing people reaches the brain through the eyes. It is important that we understand how light works to make sense of our world.

# LIGHT SOURCES

Objects that give out light are called luminous objects. They range in size from stars to microscopic animals that live in the sea.

## STARS

The most important source of light in our world is the Sun. It is a star, and like all stars it is a huge, immensely hot ball of gas. At the centre of the Sun, nuclear reactions produce huge amounts of energy. This energy passes to the Sun's surface, where it is released as light and heat.

Light from the Sun spreads out through space in all directions. Some of it reaches the Earth and gives us daylight.

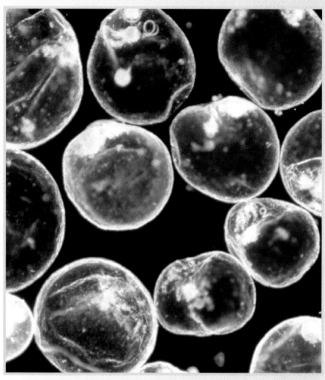

Sea sparkles (Noctiluca) are tiny animals that can produce their own light. Many other living things glow in the dark. This is known as bioluminescence.

The filament in a light bulb is made of a metal called tungsten, which can stand extreme heat without melting and produces a very bright light.

## THE LIGHT BULB

In an electric light bulb, a current of electricity pushes its way through a thin wire called a filament. As the current passes through, it transports so much energy that it releases large amounts of heat and light.

## FLAMES

When an object burns, the flames give out light. This is because when something burns, tiny particles of carbon form above the burning material. These particles then become so hot that they glow.

## SEE THE CARBON

Ask an adult to light a candle. Hold a white plate above the flame for one second and see the carbon particles (soot) settle on its surface.

## FLUORESCENCE

A fluorescent material absorbs energy and then releases some of it in the form of light. In televisions, computer screens and fluorescent lights (strip lights), there is a layer of fluorescent material. When it receives energy from a current of electricity, it gives out light.

## WHERE DOES MOONLIGHT COME FROM?

It is perhaps easy to think that the Moon is a light source like the Sun. However, the Greek philosopher Thales (624–546 BC) was not convinced.

He believed that the Moon reflected light from the Sun. Anaxagoras (500–428 BC), another Greek philosopher, agreed with Thales and worked out an explanation.

He suggested that the Moon changes shape each night because it acts as a reflector of the Sun's light.

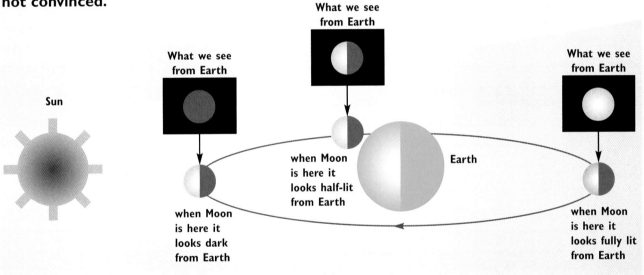

The Moon orbits the Earth once every 28 days. As it orbits, it seems to change shape because we see different amounts of the side that is lit by the Sun.

## LASER

Theodore Maiman (born 1927), an American scientist, built the first laser in 1960. Light travels in the form of tiny waves that are too small to see. In normal light these waves are jumbled together, but in a laser all the light waves are made to move in step. This produces a beam of light that can be powerful enough to cut holes in metal. Less powerful lasers can produce a very fine beam of light. Lasers are used in many ways, for instance in surgery and in CD players and to scan bar codes at supermarket checkouts.

# THE PATH OF LIGHT

We have seen that when a sunbeam shines between the clouds, the edges of the beam are straight (see page 4). This suggests that light travels in straight lines. Sunlight can reach the Earth because the air lets light pass through it. But most materials block the passage of light.

### KEEP IT STRAIGHT

Look down a bendy plastic tube at an object. You can only see the object when the tube is straight.

### LINE THEM UP

Take three pieces of card and bend them so that they can stand up. Make a hole in the centre of the two cards nearest to you. Then line them up and shine a torch onto the hole in the first card. Can you see a spot of light on the third card? What happens if the two cards with holes are not in line?

In this window you can see objects outside through the glass and objects inside reflected in the glass.

### TRANSPARENT TO LIGHT

If you shine a torch through the air, it will light up a distant surface. This means that the light has travelled or been transmitted through the air. A substance that lets light travel through it is called a transparent material.

### ALL THROUGH THE WINDOW?

When light passes from one transparent material to another, for instance from glass to air, not all the light passes through. When you are looking out of a window, light from outside travels through the air to reach the window, then passes through the window glass to reach your eyes. If you look closer at the window, you may also be able to see dim images of objects inside the room. These are reflections. Most of the light from these objects passes through the window and will be seen by people looking in, but a small amount of light reflects back to you.

## SCATTERING LIGHT

Some materials let light through, but the light rays are scattered as they pass. These materials are called translucent materials. You cannot see objects clearly through translucent materials.

When frosted glass is made, it is given a rough surface so that it becomes translucent.

Frosted glass is an example of a translucent material. It is used, for instance, in bathroom windows. Light from the bathroom passes outwards through the window but, because the light is scattered, people outside the bathroom cannot see inside very clearly.

## LIGHT STOPPERS

When light strikes most materials, it does not pass through at all. Some of the light is absorbed by the material and some is reflected away. On the side of the material away from the light there is a shadow. Materials that do not allow light to pass through them are called opaque materials. You are made mainly from opaque materials.

## SUPER-STRAIGHT BEAMS

In 1969 a reflector was set up on the Moon to measure the distance from the Earth to the Moon. A laser (see page 7) was aimed at the reflector from Earth. The light travelled in a straight line from the Earth to the Moon, hit the reflector and returned to Earth. Using the reflector, scientists have been able to discover that the Moon is moving away from the Earth at the rate of four centimetres a year.

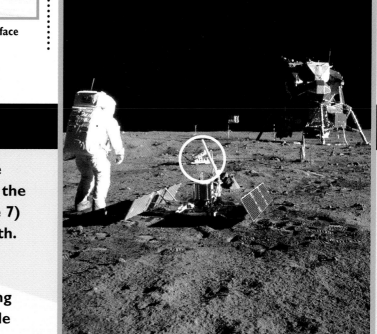

In 1969 the US astronaut Buzz Aldrin set up a laser reflector for measuring the distance from Earth to the Moon. The reflector is circled in this picture.

# SHADOWS

When light shines on an opaque object, its path is stopped. Some light is absorbed and some is reflected, but none passes through the object. On the side of the object away from the light is a dark patch – a shadow.

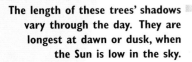
The length of these trees' shadows vary through the day. They are longest at dawn or dusk, when the Sun is low in the sky.

## SHADOW LENGTH

Every opaque object casts a shadow, but the shadow changes with the direction of the light. When light shines down on an object from above, a short shadow is cast. When light shines from the side, the object makes a longer shadow.

## PREDICT YOUR SPOOKY FACE

Shine a torch upwards in front of your chin to make a spooky face in the dark. If you do this, which parts of your face will light up and which parts will be in shadow? Test your prediction in front of a mirror.

## SHADOW AND HALF-SHADOW

A shadow provides evidence that light travels in straight lines. If you look at a shadow cast by the Sun, it has a sharp edge. If light travelled in curves or zigzags, it could bend round the object and reduce the shadow, perhaps even to nothing.

When an object is lit by a broad source of light such as a desk lamp, you sometimes see a shadow with a grey border. This half-shadow is called the penumbra, and the dark part of the shadow inside it is called the umbra. The existence of the penumbra does not mean that light bends round the object. The light rays travel in straight lines, but as they come from a broad source of light close by they overlap to make the penumbra.

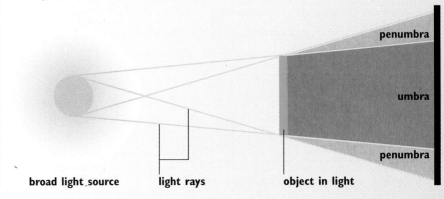
penumbra

umbra

penumbra

broad light source      light rays      object in light

## HOW DOES THE SHADOW CHANGE?

Hold a ball close to a wall and shine a torch on it from about 40 centimetres away. Move the torch right up to the ball and look for a penumbra. Now move the torch back again and this time move the ball towards the torch. Is the penumbra smaller or larger than before?

## TWO SHADOWS

We tend to think that an object has one shadow, but if two different lights shine on it, an object can have two shadows. You may think that when a large number of different lights are shining on an object it can have a large number of shadows. However, lights shining from opposite directions can cancel out each other's shadows.

A shadow puppet theatre in Bali, Indonesia.

## GIANT SHADOWS

The size of a shadow varies depending on how close an object is to the light and to the surface the shadow falls on. In a shadow puppet theatre, shadows are cast by puppets onto a screen. A puppet's shadow can be made huge by moving the puppet close to the light, or small by moving it away.

Shadows of mountains on the Moon's surface.

## UNDERSTANDING THE MOON

Galileo (1564–1642), an Italian scientist, looked at the Moon during its different phases and saw how the shadows of mountains changed. When the Moon is a thin crescent, the Sun shines across the surface casting long shadows. Around full Moon, when the Sun shines directly down on the surface, shorter shadows are cast. Galileo used his observations to work out the heights of the mountains.

# THE COLOURS IN LIGHT

If you go into your bedroom when it is dark and switch on the light, the bulb appears to give out white light. Yet all around you there are objects of many different colours. If light was just white, you would expect all the objects to appear white too. The answer is that white light is not what it seems. It is made up from all the colours we can see.

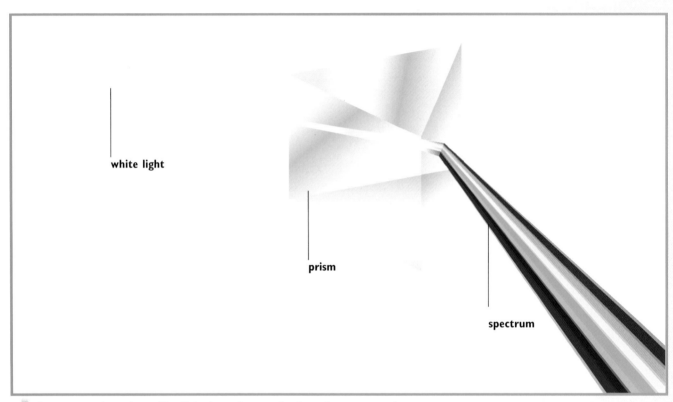

white light

prism

spectrum

One way to show that white light is a mixture of colours is to use a prism.

## SPLITTING WHITE LIGHT

A prism is a five-sided block of glass in which three of the faces form the shape of a triangle. When a beam of white light strikes one of the sides of the triangle at an angle, the light is bent (refracted). All the colours in the light are refracted, but different colours are bent by different amounts. Red light is refracted least, and blue light bends most. This results in the colours separating and spreading out to form a band of rainbow colours known as a spectrum.

## MAKE YOUR OWN SPECTRUM

Fill a straight-sided jar or tumbler with water. Cut a slit in a piece of black card then stick the card to the jar or tumbler. Place the jar or tumbler by a sunny window with the slit facing the light. Put a white sheet of paper by the jar on the opposite side to the slit and look for a spectrum.

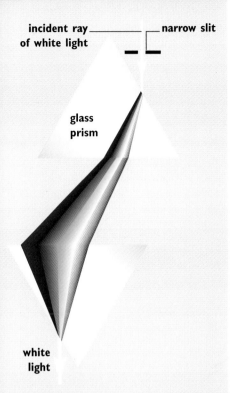

incident ray — narrow slit
of white light

glass
prism

white
light

**Isaac Newton (1642–1727), an English scientist, bought a prism at a fair. He put it in a dark room and shone sunlight through it from a hole in a window shutter. The prism split up the light into a spectrum of colours on the opposite wall.**

**It was possible that the prism could have produced the colours, so Newton got a second prism and placed it behind the first, but the opposite way round. When the coloured light from the first prism passed through the second prism, a beam of white light formed. This proved that white light was really made from light of different colours combined.**

## SEEING COLOURS

When beams of light strike a surface, often part of the light is reflected and part is absorbed. The surface may absorb some colours and reflect others. For example, a red pullover reflects red light, but absorbs all other colours in the spectrum. The pullover looks red because we see the red light reflected from its surface. Some surfaces absorb all the colours and reflect none. We see them as black. A surface that reflects all the colours is seen as white.

## FILTERS

Have you ever looked at the world through a transparent coloured sweet paper? Depending on the colour of the paper, the world looks red, blue or yellow. This is because the sweet paper acts as a light filter. A light filter lets some colours of light through and keeps back others. The colours that are kept back are absorbed by the filter.

## HOW DO THEY LOOK?

Coloured liquids can act as filters too. Look at the world through bottles of different coloured bath liquids. Look through each liquid at the other liquids. How do red liquids and blue liquids look through a green liquid?

**By studying filters and paints, you can find out more about colour.**

## COMBINED COLOURS

We saw on the previous page how a light filter absorbs some colours but allows one or two to pass through. A curious thing happens if you use red, green and blue filters to make three coloured lights, then shine the beams so that they overlap. Where all three colours combine, an area of white light appears. Red, blue and green are called the primary colours of light, because added together they make white light.

When two primary colours of light are combined, they make new colours. Red and green light in equal amounts make yellow; blue and green together make cyan (turquoise blue); and blue and red make magenta (pinkish purple). The colours that are produced when two primary colours of light mix equally are called secondary colours.

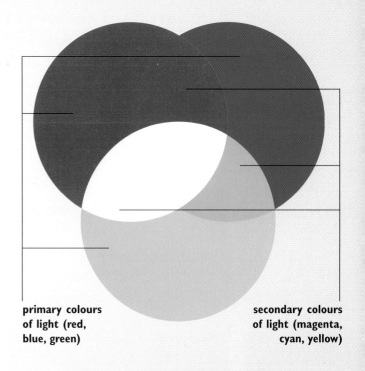

primary colours of light (red, blue, green)

secondary colours of light (magenta, cyan, yellow)

## TESTING FILTER EFFECTS

Fit a red filter to one torch and a green filter to another (you could use sweet papers as filters). Shine them both onto a white card from the same distance, so that they overlap. Now try moving one of the torches closer, then further away. How does this affect the colour on the card?

## HOW A COLOUR SCREEN WORKS

The screen of a colour television or a computer is covered in substances called phosphors, which glow when they receive a current of electricity. There are three different phosphors, which glow in the primary colours – red, blue and green. With just these three phosphors, a screen can reproduce any colour. This is done by controlling how the phosphors glow. For example, if the green glows brightly and the red glows dimly, we see a brown colour.

## PAINT COLOURS

When you paint a picture, you are colouring with paints rather than with light. Each paint contains pigments, which absorb some colours and reflect others. Green paint, for instance, absorbs all the colours in light except green, which is reflected back from the surface.

## MIXING PAINTS

Mixing paints does not give the same results as mixing coloured lights. This is because when paints mix they subtract colours from white light. Coloured light beams, in contrast, add their colours together.

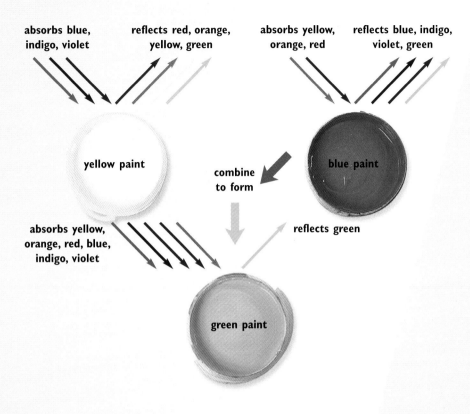

absorbs blue, indigo, violet

reflects red, orange, yellow, green

absorbs yellow, orange, red

reflects blue, indigo, violet, green

yellow paint

blue paint

combine to form

absorbs yellow, orange, red, blue, indigo, violet

reflects green

green paint

You can see how paint colours mix by looking at what happens if you mix blue and yellow paint. Blue paint absorbs yellow, red

and orange light, and reflects blue, indigo, violet and green. Yellow paint absorbs blue, indigo and violet light, but reflects red, orange, yellow and green.

If you mix the two paints together, the resulting pigment absorbs red, yellow and orange light (from the blue paint), but also blue, indigo and violet light (from the yellow paint). The only colour still reflected is green: so mixing blue and yellow paints produces green.

## PRIMARY PAINTS

There are three primary colours of paint, but they are not the same as those of light. The primary colours of paints are yellow, cyan and magenta. All the colours in the pictures in this book are made by different combinations of yellow, cyan and magenta printing inks.

**When the primary colours of paints are combined, they make black, rather than white.**

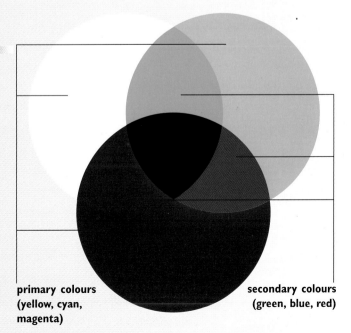

primary colours (yellow, cyan, magenta)

secondary colours (green, blue, red)

# REFLECTING LIGHT

We tend to think of reflected light as coming from mirrors, but almost every surface reflects some light. You are reflecting light right now. If this did not happen, nobody would see you! We see objects because light reflects off them and into our eyes.

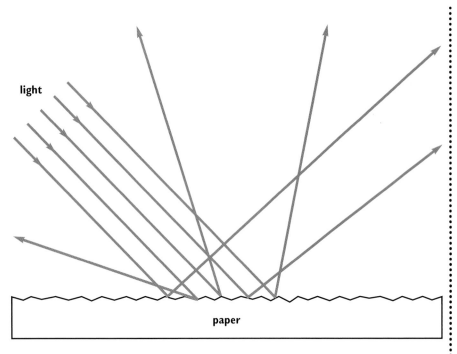

light

paper

## ROUGH REFLECTION

Most surfaces are slightly uneven or rough. When light rays strike them, they bounce off in all directions. This kind of reflection is the most common kind of reflection. It is called diffuse reflection.

When light reflects off one surface it can strike another. The light reflecting off the objects that you see around you may have been reflected many times before it enters your eyes.

## LIGHT UP YOUR HAND

Turn on a table lamp and face it. Hold up a hand and notice how the side towards you is dark. Now hold up a piece of white paper between you and your hand but facing the lamp. See how the light from the paper lights up your hand. Use a small mirror instead of the paper – how does your hand light up now?

## REFLECTIONS FROM SMOOTH SURFACES

Light shining on a very smooth surface is reflected in a special way. Instead of reflections bouncing off at all angles, the light rays reflect in a very regular pattern. This is called specular reflection. In specular reflection, a ray of light striking a surface (the incident ray) and the ray of light reflected away (the reflected ray) are related. If you measure the angle at which the incident ray strikes the surface, you will find that the reflected ray leaves the surface at the same angle but in a different direction.

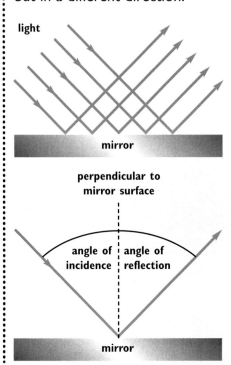

light

mirror

perpendicular to mirror surface

angle of incidence   angle of reflection

mirror

## SEEING AN IMAGE

Specular reflection from a very smooth surface allows a picture or image to appear in it. When you look in a mirror, some of the light from your face strikes the mirror, is reflected and enters your eye. As the rays are reflected in an orderly way, they form an image that seems to be behind the mirror.

Your image in a mirror looks like an exact copy of you. But in fact the mirror reverses the image from left to right. You can see this when you look at words in a mirror, which seem to be written backwards.

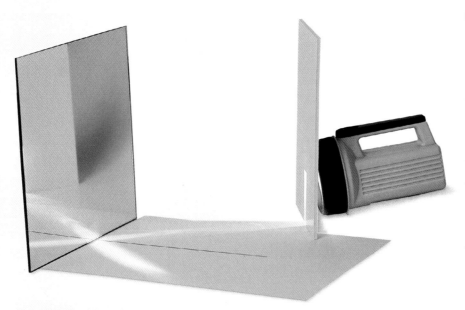

## CHECK ANGLES OF REFLECTION

Cut a slit in a piece of card and stick the card on the front of a torch. Stand a mirror on a sheet of white paper and draw a line on the paper perpendicular to the mirror's surface. Shine the torch at an angle across the paper towards the mirror, and measure the angle it makes with the line you have drawn. Now measure the angle made by the reflected ray. Are they the same?

## MIRRORS THROUGH THE AGES

A polished, glass-like rock called obsidian was used for making mirrors in Turkey about 7,500 years ago. Later, mirrors were made from polished copper or bronze. During the Middle Ages the first glass mirrors were made. A coating of tin on the back of the mirror made it shiny. Then in 1835 the German scientist Justus von Liebig (1803–1873) found a way of silvering mirrors (covering the back with a layer of pure silver). This is how mirrors are made today.

# CURVED MIRRORS

There are two kinds of curved mirror. A mirror that curves inwards, like a bowl, is called a concave mirror. A mirror that curves outwards, like a dome, is called a convex mirror. When light strikes them it is reflected in different ways. The way the light is reflected from them is best understood by looking at what happens when parallel rays of light, such as those in a torch, hit the mirror.

## CONCAVE MIRRORS

When parallel rays of light strike a concave mirror, the rays reflect off its surface and meet together at a point called the principal focus. How objects are seen in the mirror depends on where they are in relation to the principal focus. If an object is further away from the mirror than the principal focus, the mirror shows an upside-down image of it. As you move the object nearer to the principal focus the image becomes larger and even magnified, but it is still upside down. If the object is placed between the principal focus and the mirror, you see a magnified image that is the right way up.

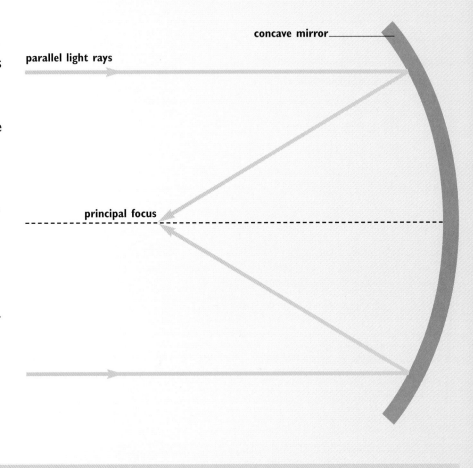

concave mirror

parallel light rays

principal focus

The reflectors in torches and car headlamps are parabolic mirrors.

## USING **CONCAVE MIRRORS**

Many concave mirrors are curved like part of the inside of a ball. If a lamp is put at their principal focus, the light from it spreads out over a wide area. A parabolic mirror is a concave mirror with a deeper curve to it. A lamp at the principal focus of this kind of mirror produces a strong, straight beam of reflected light.

convex mirror

## CONVEX MIRRORS

When parallel rays of light strike a convex mirror, the reflected rays spread out in all directions. Images of objects placed anywhere in front of the mirror appear the right way up, but smaller than the object. Light can also strike the mirror from many directions and this gives the mirror a wide field of view.

Convex mirrors have a wider field of view than flat ones. This makes them useful as security mirrors, or for rear-view mirrors in vehicles.

## LIGHT IN A LADLE

Place a large spoon or ladle at one end of a block and a torch at the other. Arrange for half of each to be above the surface of the block. Shine the torch so its light crosses the surface of the block. Move the concave surface of the spoon to find the principal focus (when the image first turns right way up). What happens when you turn the ladle round so the light shines on its convex (back) surface?

## FIGHTING WITH MIRRORS

As the Romans expanded their empire, one of their armies tried to take over the city of Syracuse on the island of Sicily. It took three years for them to complete their task. Greek writers after the event said that this was because of defences designed by Archimedes (about 287–212 BC), a Greek scientist. These defences included concave mirrors, which were used to focus sunlight onto attacking Roman ships and set them alight. Most people now think that Greek writers invented these defences to show that the Greek brains were mightier than Roman muscle. The Romans did eventually succeed in taking over the city, and during the takeover Archimedes was killed.

19

# BENDING LIGHT

**If you stand on the edge of a swimming pool and look down into the water, you may think that the pool is shallow. When you jump in, you might find that the water is deeper than you thought. The reason for this is refraction – bending of light as it moves from one transparent substance to another.**

When light travelling through a transparent substance hits the surface of another transparent substance head on, it carries on through the second substance in the same direction. However, if the light rays strike the second substance at an angle, they appear to bend and change direction. This 'bending' of light is called refraction.

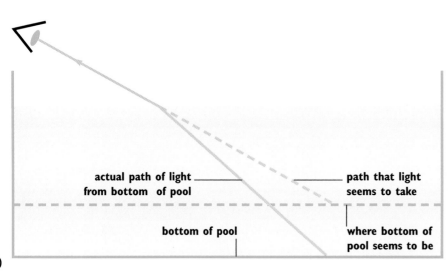

actual path of light from bottom of pool _____ _____ path that light seems to take

bottom of pool

where bottom of pool seems to be

## THAT SHALLOW SWIMMING POOL...

Refraction happens because light travels at different speeds through different transparent substances. When light rays from the bottom of a swimming pool strike the surface of the air at an angle, they speed up and bend away from the straight path they would normally take. If these light rays enter your eyes, they appear to be coming from a different place in the pool, closer to the surface. This is what makes the pool seem shallow.

## THE BENDING STRAW

Fill a tall beaker with water. Look down into the water and then lower one end of a straw into it. The straw seems to be magnified and slightly distorted due to refraction where the water and air meet. When you pull the straw out it looks normal again.

## CAN YOU SEE THE COIN?

Place a coin in a shallow bowl such as a soup bowl. Stand up straight and move back until you can no longer see the coin over the edge of the bowl. Look down and note the position of your feet. Fill the bowl with water and return to the exact same position. If you look at the bowl you should now be able to see the coin. Light rays coming from it are refracted at the water's surface and travel over the edge of the bowl, into your eyes.

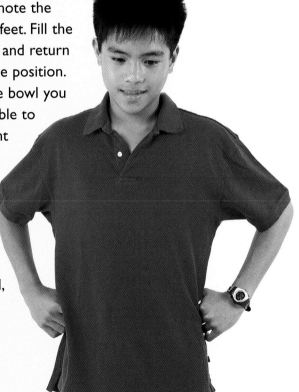

**Willebrord van Roijen Snell (1591–1626), a Dutch mathematician, worked out that there was a relationship between the angle at which a light ray struck the surface of a transparent substance and the angle at which it travelled through that substance. This relationship became known as the Law of Refraction. It helped other scientists learn more about refraction.**

## MIRRORS AND LENSES

We saw earlier (pages 16–19) how, from the study of reflection, different kinds of mirrors have been developed for a wide range of uses. Just as mirrors developed from reflection studies, so lenses developed from refraction studies. There are two basic kinds of lens – the convex lens, with sides curving outwards, and the concave lens, with sides curving inwards. Both kinds of lenses have a wide range of uses.

_____ convex lens

concave lens _____

# LENSES

You look at the world through lenses even if you do not wear glasses, because there are lenses in your eyes. A lens is an object made from transparent material that has one or both of its sides curved either inwards or outwards. As we saw on pages 18–19, there are two main kinds of lenses – convex lenses and concave lenses.

## HOW A CONVEX LENS WORKS

When a light ray strikes the middle of a convex lens head on, it passes straight through without being refracted. Light rays that strike other parts of the lens are refracted by different amounts. As they leave the lens they come together, or converge, at a point called the focus.

A magnifying glass is made from a convex lens. If you hold a magnifying glass close to something and look at it through the lens, you get a magnified view of the object.

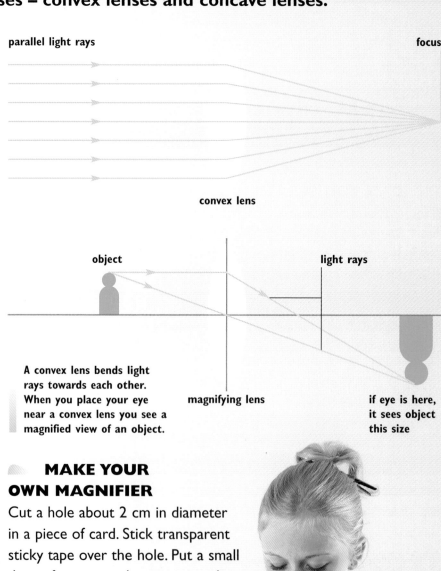

A convex lens bends light rays towards each other. When you place your eye near a convex lens you see a magnified view of an object.

### FIND THE FOCUS

Hold a magnifying glass up to a window when the Sun is not shining. Hold a piece of white card behind the magnifying glass. Move the card and glass until you can see a clear view of the window on the card. This is the point of focus. Notice that the image produced is upside down and smaller than the real window. What happens to the image if you move closer to the window again?

### MAKE YOUR OWN MAGNIFIER

Cut a hole about 2 cm in diameter in a piece of card. Stick transparent sticky tape over the hole. Put a small drop of water on the tape over the hole. Look at a coin through the drop of water. The water should behave like a lens and magnify parts of the coin.

parallel light rays

rays diverge (spread)

concave lens

A microscope is a tube with lenses at either end. At the end nearest the object to be viewed is the objective lens. This is actually a combination of lenses, designed to give a clear magnified image of the object. At the other end of the tube is the eyepiece. The lenses in the eyepiece focus and enlarge the image made by the objective lenses.

## CONCAVE LENSES

When light rays pass through a concave lens they spread out and do not come to a focus. If you were to look at these words through a concave lens, you would see them the right way up but smaller.

One very useful thing about concave lenses is that they can help to make details clearer. So they are often used in combination with convex lenses, to help clear up any details that are lost due to flaws in the convex lenses. Good telescopes and microscopes use combinations of concave and convex lenses to give high-quality images.

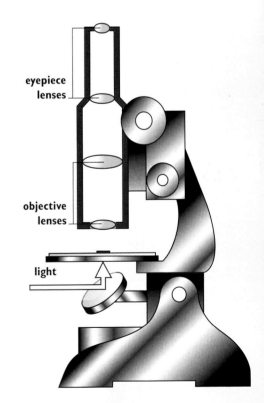

eyepiece lenses

objective lenses

light

## LENSES AND MAGNIFICATION

Alhazen (about 965–1039), a physicist from Persia (now Iran), made many discoveries about light and its behaviour. Alhazen studied lenses and found that the amount of magnification a convex lens produced was related to the way its surfaces were curved. He found that the greater the curve of the lens, the greater the magnification it produced.

# THE EYE

Imagine that you are riding on a ray of light about to enter the eye. What would your journey be like?

## JOURNEY INTO THE EYE

The first thing you would meet as you reached the eye would be a thin, transparent membrane called the conjunctiva. Then you would pass through a curved, transparent structure called the cornea. Here the light would be refracted inwards. You would pass through the eye's black hole – the pupil – then on through the lens, where the light would be refracted again. Finally you would pass through the transparent jelly that fills most of the eye, before striking the retina.

The retina is the light-sensitive surface at the back of the eye. It is made up of millions of tiny cells. Some are rod-shaped and are sensitive to dim light. These rod cells allow us to see a little in the dark. Other cells are cone-shaped and are sensitive to different colours. These cone cells work only in bright light.

## MAKING AN IMAGE

Light rays entering the eye come to a focus on the retina and create an image of what the eye can see. The rods and cones fire off messages that pass along nerves to the brain. Here, in a special area at the back of the head, is the brain's visual centre. This helps us to make sense of the things our eyes see. For example, it turns the inverted image on the retina the right way up.

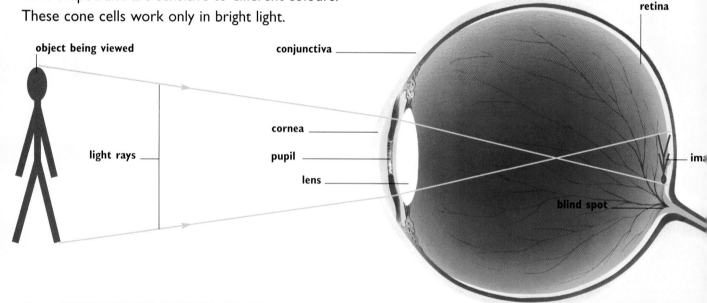

object being viewed · conjunctiva · cornea · pupil · lens · light rays · retina · ima[ge] · blind spot

## FIND YOUR BLIND SPOT

There is one area at the back of the eye that is not sensitive to light. It is called the blind spot. It is the place where nerve fibres from all the retina cells join to form the optic nerve. Hold up this book about 30 cm in front of you. Close your right eye, and with your left eye look at the red dot on the right. Keep looking at the red dot and very slowly bring the book closer to your face. At some point the blue cross will disappear as light from it falls on your blind spot.

Alhazen (see page 23) was the first to recognise that light rays enter the eye from the objects around us, rather than the eye seeing by sending out rays, as the Greek philosopher Empedocles (about 490–430 BC) had believed. Later, Johannes Kepler (AD 1571–1630), a German scientist, went on to explain how light refracted within the eye to form an image on the retina. He was also the first person to work out how lenses could be used to correct short and long sight (see below).

## CORRECTING SHORT AND LONG SIGHT

The two most common problems people have with their eyes are short sight and long sight. Short sight is caused by the lens in the eye focusing light in front of the retina instead of on it. Long sight is caused by the lens focusing light behind the retina.

These two defects can be corrected by spectacles or contact lenses. A kind of concave lens called a diverging lens is used to correct short sight. It spreads out the light rays a little before they enter the eye, and this helps to focus them on the retina. Long sight is corrected using a convex or converging lens. This brings the light rays together a little before they enter the eye.

### SHORT SIGHT

eye cannot focus on distant objects

diverging lens spreads light

image focused on retina

### LONG SIGHT

eye cannot focus on close objects

converging lens bends light

image focused on retina

# CAPTURING LIGHT

Close your eyes, then open your right eye and close it again quickly. Your right eye has just behaved like a camera. When you opened it, light flooded in and the lens focused light on the retina. When you take a photograph, light floods into the camera and a lens focuses the rays onto a light-sensitive surface. The end result is a photograph.

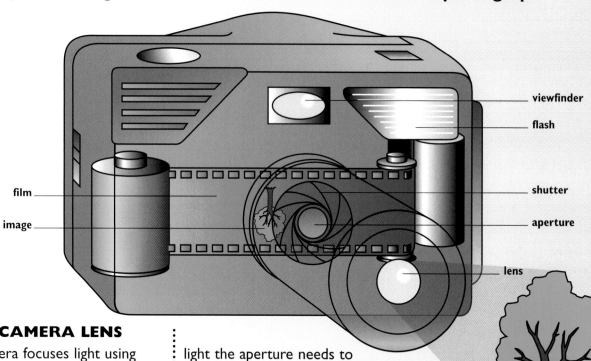

viewfinder

flash

film

image

shutter

aperture

lens

object

## THE CAMERA LENS

A camera focuses light using a lens. A camera lens can only focus images that are a certain distance away. If the subject of a picture is too close or too far away, the picture is blurred. Many cameras get round this problem by having a lens that can move outwards or inwards. This allows the camera to focus on objects that are close by or further away.

## LETTING IN LIGHT

Behind the lens is a hole called the aperture, which can change to let more or less light into the camera. In dim conditions the aperture needs to be large to let in plenty of light. In bright

light the aperture needs to be small, because too much light can spoil the picture.

To get a nice sharp image, light has to be let in for only a short time. The camera's shutter makes sure this happens. For most pictures, the shutter opens for about 1/30th to 1/50th of a second. But for fast-moving action photos, the shutter has to open for a much shorter time – 1/500th of a second or less – or the movement will be blurred.

## PHOTOGRAPHIC FILM

Photographic film is a sheet of plastic, covered with a layer of tiny, light-sensitive crystals.

When you take a picture, light is focused on the film and changes these crystals. They go darker or lighter, or change colour, to make an image of what the camera sees. The image on a film is a negative: light areas of the picture are dark, and dark areas are light. Light is shone through the negative onto light-sensitive paper to make a print.

## DIGITAL CAMERAS

Instead of using film, a digital camera has thousands of tiny photocells. The cells produce electrical signals that record the amount and colour of light falling on them. The signals from all the photocells together make an electronic copy of the image the camera sees. This is stored in the camera's memory. It can later be displayed on a screen, or printed to make a photograph.

With a digital camera, you see the picture on a screen before you take it.

## MAKE A PINHOLE CAMERA

Take a cardboard box (such as a shoe box), and cut a large square hole in each end. Make a tiny, neat pinhole in a piece of thick aluminium foil (for example a foil baking tray). Tape the foil over the hole at one end of the box, and greaseproof paper over the other end.

Look at the greaseproof paper to see the pinhole picture. How does it compare with the real view?

## THE FIRST **PHOTOGRAPHERS**

Joseph Niépce (1765–1833), a French inventor, focused light onto a metal plate covered in light-sensitive chemicals to make the first ever photograph. The light had to be shone onto the chemical for eight hours to make a picture. Louis Daguerre (1789–1851), another French inventor, developed a much faster process, which took only a minute to make a picture.

27

# THE SPEED OF LIGHT

When you switch on an electric lamp in a dark room, light seems to appear instantly. This means it must be travelling very, very fast indeed. Sound travels pretty fast – it covers about a kilometre every 3 seconds. We can see that light travels much faster than this by looking at thunder and lightning.

Thunder is the noise that lightning makes when it flashes through the air.

## THUNDER AND LIGHTNING

When there is a flash of lightning in a storm, a rumble of thunder happens at the same time. If the lightning happens close by, you see the lightning and hear the thunder together. But if the lightning is at a distance, you see it first, then hear the thunder. The light reaches your eyes almost instantly, but the thunder takes several seconds to reach your ears.

## HOW FAR IS THE STORM

Next time there is a storm, use the difference in speeds between light and sound to work out how far away the storm is. Watch out for a lightning flash, then time how long afterwards you hear the thunder. Sound takes about three seconds to travel one kilometre. So if you time the gap between seeing the lightning and hearing the thunder, then divide it by three, you will know how many kilometres away the storm is.

## THE FASTEST THERE IS

Light is not just fast – it is the fastest thing there is. The great physicist Albert Einstein (1879–1955) worked out that the speed of light is constant, and that nothing can go faster.

So how fast does light travel? When rockets fly into space, they travel at over 11 kilometres per second (about 25,000 miles per hour). However, compared to light speed, the rocket is hardly moving! Light travels at 300 million metres per second (670 billion miles per hour). If you could travel at light speed, you could reach the Moon in just over a second and the Sun in about eight minutes.

By the middle of the 19th century, scientists thought that light moved as waves of electricity and magnetism linked together (electromagnetic waves). James Clerk Maxwell (1831–1879), a Scottish scientist, calculated that if light was made up of tiny electromagnetic waves, it should move at 300 million metres per second.

Armand Fizeau (1819–1896), a French scientist, invented a complicated machine with a mirror and a rapidly turning cogwheel to measure the speed of light. He used it to calculate that light travelled at 314,262,944 metres per second. Later, other scientists, including the Frenchman Leon Foucault (1819–1868), developed Fizeau's experiment and found that the speed of light matched Clerk Maxwell's original calculations.

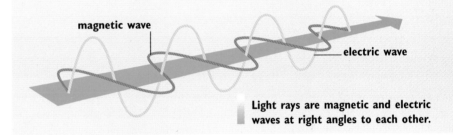

magnetic wave

electric wave

Light rays are magnetic and electric waves at right angles to each other.

When we see the Andromeda Galaxy in the sky, we are seeing light that has travelled for 2 million years before reaching our eyes.

## ACROSS THE UNIVERSE

Distances between stars and galaxies are so huge that kilometres are too small to measure them. So astronomers use a unit of measurement called the light year. This is the distance that light travels in a year – 9.5 billion kilometres. Astronomers have worked out the distances of many stars and galaxies from Earth. For example, the bright star Sirius is nine light years away from Earth. The Andromeda Galaxy, which can just be seen on a clear night, is just over two million light years away.

# TIMELINE

**Thales (624–546 BC)**, a Greek philosopher, proposed that the Moon reflected light from the Sun and was not a source of light.

**Anaxagoras (about 500–428 BC)**, a Greek philosopher, suggested that the changing shape of the Moon each night was due to the way the Moon reflected the Sun's light.

**Empedocles (about 490–430 BC)**, a Greek philosopher, believed that the eyes sent out rays to help us see.

**Archimedes (about 287–212 BC)**, a Greek scientist, is said to have used concave mirrors to focus sunlight onto attacking Roman ships and set them alight.

**Alhazen (about 965–1039)**, a mathematician and physicist from Persia (now Iran), made many discoveries about light and its behaviour.

**Galileo (1564–1642)**, an Italian scientist, used the shadows cast by mountains on the Moon to calculate the heights of these mountains.

**Johannes Kepler (1571–1630)**, a German scientist, was the first to discover how light was refracted in the eye.

**Willebrord van Roijen Snell (1580–1626)**, a Dutch mathematician, worked out the Law of Refraction.

**Isaac Newton (1642–1727)**, an English scientist, used a prism to show that white light was made up from all the colours we can see.

**Jan Ingenhousz (1730–1799)**, a Dutch scientist, showed that plants take in carbon dioxide and give out oxygen when light shines on them.

**Joseph-Nicéphore Niépce (1765–1833)**, a French inventor, took the first photograph; it took eight hours for the light to make a picture.

**Louis Daguerre (1789–1851)**, a French inventor, developed a process for taking a photograph that only took one minute.

**James Clerk Maxwell (1831–1879)**, a Scottish scientist, correctly calculated that light travels at a speed of 300,000,000 metres per second.

**Justus von Liebig (1803–1873)**, a German scientist, invented the method of silvering mirrors that is used today.

**Armand Fizeau (1819–1896)**, a French scientist, measured the speed of light as 314,262,944 metres per second.

**Leon Foucault (1819–1868)**, a French scientist, measured the speed of light in water and found that it was slower than the speed in air.

**Albert Einstein (1879–1955)**, a German-born American physicist, said that the speed of light was constant, and that nothing could go faster.

**Theodore Maiman (born 1927)**, an American scientist, built the first laser in 1960.

# GLOSSARY

**concave** – having a surface shaped like the inside of a bowl.

**convex** – having a surface shaped like the outside of a ball.

**energy** – the ability of things to perform work such as movement.

**filament** – a very thin piece of wire used in a light bulb.

**fluorescence** – when a material absorbs energy, then gives some of it out as light.

**focus** – to bring light waves together at a point.

**image** – a picture produced when light rays are reflected from a mirror or focused by a lens.

**incident ray** – a ray of light striking an object.

**laser** – a kind of light that produces a concentrated, very thin beam of light of a single colour.

**lens** – a shaped piece of glass or other transparent material that refracts (bends) light in a particular way.

**material** – any kind of substance.

**opaque** – describes a substance that does not allow light to pass through.

**parabolic mirror** – a concave mirror with a deep curve to it.

**parallel** – when two or more objects are lying or, in the case of light beams, moving side by side at the same distance from each other all along their length.

**penumbra** – the lighter area that is found at the edges of a fuzzy shadow.

**perpendicular** – at right angles.

**primary colours** (light) – the three colours that when mixed equally make white light. They are red, blue and green.

**primary colours** (paint) – the three colours that when mixed equally make black paint. They are yellow, cyan and magenta.

**prism** – a five-sided block of glass with two identical triangular faces positioned opposite each other that can be used to split white light.

**refraction** – when light bends as it moves from one transparent substance into another.

**reflected ray** – a ray of light reflected from a mirror or some other surface.

**reflection** – when light bounces off the surface of an object.

**secondary colours** – the colours produced by the equal mixing of two primary colours.

**spectrum** – a rainbow of colours produced when white light is split by a prism.

**specular reflection** – when light bounces off a surface in a regular way, as off a mirror.

**translucent** – describes a substance that allows light to pass through but is only partly see-through.

**transmitted** – passed from one place to another.

**transparent** – describes a substance that allows light to travel through it.

**umbra** – a shadow or the dark part of a shadow.

# INDEX

**Alhazen** 23, 25, 30
**Anaxagoras** 7, 30
**aperture** 26
**Archimedes** 19, 30

**bioluminescence** 6
**blind spot** 24

**camera** 26
    digital 27
    pinhole 27
**candle** 6, 24
**colours** 5, 12, 13, 14, 15, 27
    primary 14, 15
    secondary 14, 15
**concave** 18, 19, 21, 22, 23, 25
**conjunctiva** 24
**convex** 18, 19, 21, 22, 23, 25
**cornea** 24

**Daguerre, Louis** 27, 30

**Einstein, Albert** 29, 30
**eyes** 5, 8, 16, 17, 20, 21, 22, 24-25, 28, 29
**electricity** 6, 7, 14, 27, 28, 29

**filters** 13, 14
**Fizeau, Armand** 29, 30
**flames** 6, 24
**flourescence** 7
**focus** 18, 22, 23, 24, 25, 26, 27
**Foucault, Leon** 29, 30

**galaxies** 29
**Galileo** 11, 30
**glass** 4, 8, 12

**Ingenhousz, Jan** 5, 30

**Kepler, Johannes** 25, 30

**lasers** 7, 9
**lenses** 21, 22, 23, 24, 25, 26
**light**
    beams 4, 5, 7, 8, 12, 14, 15, 18
    bulb 6, 12
    energy 4, 5, 6, 7
    rays 10, 16, 17, 18, 19, 20, 21, 22, 23, 24, 25, 26, 29
    sources 4, 6, 7
    speed 20, 28, 29
    waves 4, 7, 29
    white 5, 12, 13, 14, 15
    years 29
**lightning** 28
**luminous** 6

**magnification** 18, 21, 22, 23
**Maiman, Theodore** 7
**Maxwell, James Clerk** 29, 30
**microscopes** 23
**mirrors** 5, 10, 16, 17, 18, 19, 21, 29
**Moon** 4, 7, 9, 11, 29

**Newton, Isaac** 13, 30
**Niépce, Joseph** 27, 30
**nuclear reaction** 6

**opaque** 9, 10
**optic nerve** 24

**paints** 14, 15
**parabolic mirror** 18
**penumbra** 10, 11
**photographs** 26, 27
**photosynthesis** 5
**pigment** 15

**plants** 4, 5
**principal focus** 18, 19
**prisms** 12, 13
**pupil** 24

**rainbows** 5, 12
**reflection** 4, 5, 7, 8, 9, 10, 13, 15, 16, 17, 18, 21
**reflection, diffuse** 16
**reflection, specular** 16, 17
**refraction** 4, 5, 12, 20, 21, 22, 24, 25
**retina** 24, 25, 26

**shadow** 9, 10, 11
**sight** 5, 16, 24, 25
    long 25
    short 25
**spectrum** 12, 13
**stars** 4, 6, 29
**Sun** 4, 5, 6, 7, 10, 11, 22, 29
**sunlight** 4, 5, 8, 13, 19

**telescope** 23
**Thales** 7
**thunder** 28
**translucent** 9
**transparent** 4, 8, 13, 20, 21, 22, 24
**tungsten** 6

**umbra** 10

**van Roijen Snell, Willebrord** 21, 30
**von Liebig, Justus** 17, 30

**water** 4, 5, 12, 20, 21, 22